BREAKING THE CODE

Understanding the Book of Revelation

LEADER'S GUIDE

by Donn Downall

Abingdon Press
Nashville

BREAKING THE CODE:
Understanding the Book of Revelation
LEADER'S GUIDE
by Donn Downall

Library of Congress Cataloging-in-Publication Data

Downall, Donn.
  Breaking the code : understanding the book of Revelation : leader's guide / by Donn Downall.
    p.   cm.
  Leader's guide to the book and videotape of the same title authored by Bruce Manning Metzger.
  ISBN 0-687-76973-6 (alk. paper)
  1. Bible. N.T. Revelation—Study and teaching. I. Metzger, Bruce Manning. Breaking the code. II. Title.
BS2825.5.D69   1993
228'.06—dc20   93-32696
                                                                        CIP

ISBN 13: 978-0-687-49779-9

CONTENTS

Plans for Eight Video Lessons

LESSON ONE

PURPOSE

To appreciate and understand the Book of Revelation as a carefully written document that used symbolism and code language to reinforce for Christians long ago a commitment to be faithful in spite of the brutal oppression they were enduring.

SUGGESTED PROCEDURE

If class members are not acquainted with one another, have them introduce themselves and respond briefly to a question such as, "When you were a young child, first grade or younger, what puzzled you or frightened you about the Bible?" Suggest that class members take notes during Dr. Metzger's video presentations, or write in the margins of the book as they read. Learners need ways to retain their own points of interest and questions to ponder. Remind them of an Asian proverb, "The faintest ink is more lasting than the strongest memory."

Ask learners to open their Bibles to the first chapter of Revelation. Use a reader or readers to present aloud four segments of that chapter. Mention that the readings differ somewhat from the sequence in which they appear in the Bible:

Revelation 1:9-11
Revelation 1:4-8
Revelation 1:10-20 (repeating verses 10 and 11 from first reading)
Revelation 1:1-3

Call attention to "the one who reads aloud" and "those who hear"(verse 3). Ask someone to find in *Breaking the Code*, page 22, several reasons why reading aloud was specifically mentioned.

Draw a horizontal line on chalkboard or newsprint. (If none is available, stand with your arms outstretched.) Point out the two "far ends." Mention that some Christians are at one end, avoiding the Book of Revelation as much as they can. At the other extreme are those who are so enamored by the Book of Revelation that they pay more attention to it than to the Sermon on the Mount, the Book of Psalms, or other key portions of Scripture.

Ask if any members of the group believe themselves to be at one extreme or the other. Invite them to explain why they think so.

At this point allow 17 minutes to watch
Video Lesson One if it is available.

In Dr. Metzger's book, on pages 17-18, he writes about the "literary genre" of Revelation. Ask someone to find what he calls the two basic features of most apocalypses.

Remind the group that Dr. Metzger offered three presuppositions to help persons understand this unique book of Scripture. Invite class members to try to recall these presuppositions:

1. We should take seriously what the author says; for example, when John said he had a vision, we need to accept it as a vision.
2. John used the language of symbolism to describe his visions; therefore, John's word-pictures need to be understood as symbolic representations of the divine Word received by John.
3. We should not assume that the sequence in which John received or wrote the visions has to be the order in which the content of the visions must be fulfilled; evidence seems to suggest that John sometimes stopped to review or to repeat an earlier thought.

The third presupposition leads to a frequently raised question:

Is the Book of Revelation a calendar or timeline that reveals the future?

Two statements about Jesus Christ may influence the way we answer that question:

1. Jesus Christ will return to earth after certain events happen.
2. Jesus Christ is with God's people now. (See Matthew 18:20.)

Remind the group members that it is possible for both these statements to be true. Individuals, however, may think one statement is more important than the other. Ask for a show of hands to indicate which statement group members consider more important.

Review Dr. Metzger's remarks about Revelation 1:20, "the seven lampstands are the seven churches." Why does he remind us that in

Revelation 1:13 we find Christ "in the midst of the lampstands"? Encourage comments or questions by class members.

If time is available, seek from class members responses to this key question, which will be included in some form in each lesson:

What message do you find in this passage for you or for your congregation?

You may also wish to consider this additional discussion topic if there is time:

Notice the wording of Revelation 1:9. How is it possible to share "persecution" and "the kingdom" at the same time?

POINTERS FOR LEADERS: THE APOCALYPTIC GENRE

Class members may not be familiar with the term *genre*, (ZHON-ruh), a French word referring to a particular type or category of literature. On page 17 Dr. Metzger mentions several other writings in the apocalyptic genre, and identifies two common features of all such writings. Political realities often made code language necessary to keep oppressors from understanding the writing if it should fall into their hands. For instance, the woman called "Babylon" is a code word for Rome, a city built on seven hills. (See Revelation 17:9.)

Close by asking someone (who has agreed in advance) to offer a prayer, or use the following prayer:

God, we seek to understand you better through your Word. Today we have begun to think about some puzzling words. Help us appreciate one another as you appreciate us. When we question ideas and disagree with one another or with the lecturer, remind us that we are sometimes wrong. You know when we are wrong. We admit that we are often wrong, even though we never can say, "At this moment I am wrong." Forgive us, keep us humble, and because of your love for us help us grow in our love for your Word, for one another, and for your Son Jesus Christ.

LESSON TWO

PURPOSE

To become acquainted with the Book of Revelation's seven messages to seven churches and find in them meaning for congregations today.

SUGGESTED PROCEDURE

Begin today by calling attention to the messages to seven churches in Revelation 2 and 3. Assign each class member **one** of the seven. Have them locate and read aloud the part of their message that comes after each of these phrases (each is repeated seven times):

> These are the words of . . .
> I know . . .
> Let anyone who has an ear . . .

This activity ought to call attention to the careful literary work that is found in the Book of Revelation. The planned repetition, seven varied and imaginative descriptions of the heavenly Christ, and the precise identifications of each church's strengths and weaknesses are all indications of the talent of the author.

Turn to Dr. Metzger's book, pages 29-30 for further discussion of the literary structure of the seven messages to the churches.

Allow 14 minutes at this point to watch Video Lesson Two
if it is available. Check with participants from last week to see
if the sound volume, the seating, or the lighting was right.
Total darkness is not necessary for watching a video.

Assign each of the seven messages in Revelation 2 and 3 to at least one person. (Two of the messages could be combined for a smaller group.) Ask that the messages be read silently, then that the readers respond to the key question:

What message do you find in this passage for you or for your congregation?

If time permits, consider this additional discussion question:

In Revelation 2 and 3 who are the conquerors?

Discuss any leftover questions from last week as well as the class members' responses today.

Remind the group that on the video Dr. Metzger quotes the Scottish Bible scholar, William Barclay: "A lukewarm Christian has no claim to be a Christian at all."

Draw a rough version of a Fahrenheit thermometer, showing the boiling point, 212 degrees; freezing point, 32 degrees; and three or four numbers in between, such as 50, 100, and 150. Invite each class member mentally to place himself or herself on the scale.

POINTERS FOR LEADERS: THE BRANCH DAVIDIAN TRAGEDY

On the videotape Dr. Metzger says, "The presence of Christ departs when well-intentioned people, zealous to find the right way, depart from the ultimate way which is love." You may wish to relate his words to the tragedy at the Branch Davidian compound.

Ask if any or all of the Branch Davidians were well-intentioned. Were they zealous? Had they departed from "the ultimate way which is love"? At what point? What was their reason for stockpiling vast quantities of weapons and ammunition? Viewers may want to talk about this unfortunate example of human destruction. If so, remind them that the message to the church at Ephesus includes these words: "You have tested those who claim to be apostles, but are not, and have found them to be false" (Revelation 2:2). Ask how many in your group think of the Branch Davidians as false apostles, and how many do not. Invite class members to explain their positions.

POINTERS FOR LEADERS: CHURCHES IN SEVEN CITIES

Class members may be interested in what is known about the seven churches other than what is found in the Book of Revelation. Only three are mentioned elsewhere in the New Testament. Ephesus is the best known, receiving major attention in Acts 18—20, and in several of Paul's letters (including, of course, the Letter to the Ephesians).

An important woman in the early church, Lydia, is usually associated with Philippi, where Paul met her. Acts 16:14 tells us she was originally from Thyatira.

A bit of mystery surrounds the church at Laodicea. It is mentioned several times by Paul in his Letter to the Colossians. He said he sent a letter to Laodicea. He wanted the two letters to be exchanged so that both congregations would hear both letters (Colossians 4:16).

Was Paul's letter to the Laodiceans been lost? When he wrote to Philemon, he addressed the letter to a man named Archippus, as well. Archippus is to be given a special message by the Colossians (4:17). Also, near the end of both letters, Philemon and Colossians, Paul named the same five companions, who joined him in sending greetings.

The other four churches that received messages in Revelation are mentioned nowhere else in the New Testament.

To bring the lesson to a close offer the following prayer or similar thoughts:

> **Lord, you can see our hidden selves and hear our unspoken thoughts, you know the temperature of our faith, when we are frozen Christians and when we are steaming with desire to serve our Savior. Kindle through the Scriptures the fire that can warm our hearts, we pray in Jesus' name.**

LESSON THREE

PURPOSE

To recognize and appreciate how symbolism helps us grasp abstract concepts, such as our idea of heaven, and to consider the role of Christ in God's eternal plan for humans who seek to be faithful and obedient to their Lord.

SUGGESTED PROCEDURE

Ask the group members to find Revelation 4 in their Bibles. Ask one-third of the group to read aloud the first sentence (ending with "a door stood open"). Ask another third to read aloud the next sentence (ending with "what must take place after this"). Ask the last third to read verse 2 that ends with the words "one seated on the throne" (verse 2).

Invite each class member to try to picture, in his or her mind's eye, what the "one" looked like. (Note, when ready, that the one is not described as having the form or shape of any creature, human or animal, large or small, male or female. Instead, this one seems to resemble colored lights or shining jewels.) Ask the group members to let their mind's eye again picture the words of the Scripture.

Read 4:3-11 aloud. Then ask everyone to read together the song in verse 11. Point out that the song makes clear that the one on the throne is God.

Then ask the group to turn to 5:9 and read aloud another song that begins with the same words, "You are worthy." Go back to the beginning of Revelation 5. Point out that God holds a scroll fastened with seven seals, and that no one is found who can open the seals until the coming of a lion is announced (the Lion of the tribe of Judah). But instead comes a Lamb. Ask, "Who is the Lamb?" (The answer: Jesus Christ.)

At this point in today's lesson ask each member of the class to talk to one other person about the key question:

What message do you find in this passage for you or for your congregation?

The pairs of learners will not need to report to the total class unless they desire to do so.

At this point take 17 minutes to watch
Video Lesson Three if it is available.

Ask class members if they remember what Dr. Metzger referred to as a change of location between Revelation 3 and Revelation 4.

In the second paragraph of chapter 5 in *Breaking the Code* (page 47), the meaning of the words, "Come up here," is explained. (Revelation 2 and 3 were focused on this earth, specifically on seven communities, and the church in each of them. In Revelation 4 and 5 the focus changes to heaven.)

Jot down on the chalkboard or on paper brief descriptions of how class members would describe heaven. ("Streets of gold," "many mansions," "beyond the sunset," are some possible phrases.)

Suggest that each person look in the Bible to see how John describes heaven in Revelation 4:2-7. What is mentioned first? What does the central place of the throne suggest about God? Are class members comfortable with the idea of God sitting on a throne?

Ask the group to mention other images of God that the Bible gives us. (shepherd, rock, and so forth) Ask if it makes a difference how God is described when we think of God welcoming us to heaven. Encourage the class members to talk of what they picture heaven to be.

If time permits, consider these additional discussion questions:

What do the songs, such as Revelation 4:8-11 and 5:9-14, suggest about the kind of singing done in the early church? How can Christ be the Lion of the tribe of Judah and the slaughtered Lamb at the same time? (See Revelation 5:5-6.)

Dismiss the group with this prayer:

O God our help and our eternal home, we thank you for the words of our Bible that help us keep our imaginations working. The man of Patmos described you as Holy, Holy, Holy. We know that you are three times better than the best we can imagine. As we continue to study your Revelation to John, let his astonishing words enter freely into our minds that we may stretch our wonder and our praise, through Jesus Christ the Lamb of God.

LESSON FOUR

PURPOSE

To increase our understanding of the style and function of apocalyptic literature and begin to clarify how God's gift of free will allows human beings either creative faithfulness, which brings God's rewards, or sinful usurpation of divine power, which brings God's judgment.

SUGGESTED PROCEDURE

Select four readers to read aloud the following verses from Revelation 6 as group members follow in their Bibles:

6:1-2
6:3-4
6:5-6
6:7-8

When the readers have finished, ask how many class members have heard of this particular vision before. What have they understood it to mean? Take a few minutes to discuss the key question:

What message do you find in this passage for you or for your congregation?

Make note of points for further discussion after the presentation by Dr. Metzger.

At this time turn on Video Lesson Four if you have it available. The time required is 16 minutes.

Ask three readers each to find in their Bibles one of the following passages:

Revelation 4:6-8
Ezekiel 1:4-14
Isaiah 6:1-8

On the chalkboard write the headings for three columns:
LIVING CREATURES   HORSE   RIDER

Ask class members to listen to the three readings, then be ready to help complete a chart based on Revelation 6:1-8. Explain that we find similar references (to "living creatures" or "seraphs") in each of these books of the Bible. Compare what these accounts tell us about the appearance and the roles of the "living creatures." (They sing God's praises, attend to God's wishes, and guard and use God's purifying fire.)

Ask a class member to read the verses about the first horse and rider (6:1-2) as you write on the chart:

	LIVING CREATURES	HORSE	RIDER
1.	voice of thunder; calls "Come!"	white	bow and crown conquest

Continue to fill in the chart for the other three:

2.	Come!	red	sword; slaughter
3.	Come!	black	scales; economic depression
4.	Come!	pale green (color of decaying flesh)	named Death; sword; famine; pestilence; wild animals

Discuss insights and questions about this vision of the four horsemen. Ask if class members think that their importance in the Book of Revelation may have been exaggerated by readers in recent centuries. Consider if the four living creatures, whose roles are positive, not destructive, may offer more meaning for our faith.

Turn to page 51 in *Breaking the Code* and identify what Dr. Metzger describes as the function of the four living creatures.

Discuss class members' ideas about what causes conquest, bloodshed, inflation, and other social evils. Then mention these words of Dr. Metzger from the tape, "God does not approve of famine and death and hell, **but . . .**"

Ask, "But what?" Then repeat the entire sentence as Dr. Metzger stated it: "God does not approve of famine and death and hell, but they are what must follow if people persist in opposing God's rule."

Remind the group that Dr. Metzger compares what happens when we ignore a physical law and step off a cliff with the disasterous consequences of ignoring God's moral laws.

Discuss what Dr. Metzger has to say on page 57 of his book about power and free will.

If time permits, consider these additional discussion questions:

What images are used in Revelation 7:15-17 to describe the bliss of the redeemed in glory? Do they have any special meaning for persecuted believers?

POINTERS FOR LEADERS: ARTISTS, WRITERS, AND REVELATION

The videotapes for *Breaking the Code* make use of brief glimpses of artists' interpretations of scenes described in Revelation. Each painting or sketch is the work of a particular artist from a particular cultural background and a particular time in history. They serve in the videos to provide changes of visual foreground, and are not meant to suggest "correct" imagery to match the words of John of Patmos as Dr. Metzger interprets them. A list of the art and photographs used in the video appears on page 31 of this guide.

If class members have a special interest in art that relates to the Book of Revelation, you may wish to consult a high school or college teacher of art. Such a person could give you ideas to help explain how art masterpieces relate to various parts of the Bible, especially the imaginative apocalyptic sections. You may wish to invite the art instructor to visit a session of your group.

Two books listed on page 29 of this guide emphasize Revelation's influence on the fine arts. *Mysterious Apocalypse* by Arthur Wainwright is worth examining for its art. If class members are interested in drawing connections between apocalyptic parts of the Bible and contemporary literature, you may suggest consulting selected entries in *A Dictionary of Biblical Tradition in English Literature*, edited by D.L. Jeffrey.

As a prayer to close the session you may wish to use these words:

Too often, O God of righteousness, we have limited our tears and anger to pain that has touched us or may touch us in the future. Forgive us. Remind us that your love for your creation is "like the wideness of the sea." Help us be faithful to you, and make us confident that you are Lord of all the universe and of all that will face your children throughout this life and throughout the vastness of eternity. We pray through him who continues to give us glimpses of his victory, Jesus Christ our Lord.

LESSON FIVE

PURPOSE

To realize through the vivid and horrible symbolism of the Book of Revelation that divine judgment does not mean that God desires to inflict vengeance, rather that God wills to bring people to repentance.

SUGGESTED PROCEDURE

Begin this session by asking if anyone has ever been in a swarm of locusts. If so, allow time for a brief description of what it was like. Ask class members to close their Bibles except for someone who will read aloud 9:3 through 9:10. With Bibles still closed, see how much the group can remember of the description of the locusts. After a few moments, have them open their Bibles and check their memories against the actual text.

A devastating natural disaster such as swarming locusts could have been experienced by John and at least some of his readers. Their familiarity with disasters probably made the descriptive language of Revelation even more vivid.

Invite the learners to check page 64 of *Breaking the Code* to be reminded of a major catastrophe that hit the Roman world in A.D. 79. Ask how the memories or reports of that event might have influenced John's "disciplined imagination."

Dr. Metzger has so far taken us through eleven of the twenty-two chapters in the Book of Revelation. At this halfway point a review of certain features will be valuable. If class members each have a Bible, they will be able to see the progression in the outline that follows. If not, use your Bible and the chalkboard.

Seven in Revelation 1—4 - messages to churches
Seven in Revelation 5:1-4 - seals that can be opened by no one but the Lamb:
Revelation 6:1 - first seal, first horse and rider
Revelation 6:3 - second seal, second horse and rider
Revelation 6:5 - third seal, third horse and rider

Revelation 6:7 - fourth seal, fourth horse and rider
Revelation 6:9 - fifth seal, martyrs sheltered beneath altar
Revelation 6:12-17 - sixth seal, great earthquake
Revelation 8:1 - seventh seal, a half-hour of silence in heaven

At this point mention that Dr. Metzger in today's presentation says that the next series of sevens comes in rapid-fire order: seven angels blowing seven trumpets.

You might mention that the use of "seven" in John's writing is not always obvious. Dr. Metzger points out (*Breaking the Code*, page 22) seven "beatitudes." (See page 30 of this guide.)

If you have Video Lesson Five available, allow
15 minutes to show it now. Suggest that the group
be alert for an answer to this question: "To what Old Testament events
does Dr. Metzger compare the plagues visited on God's enemies when
the trumpet sounds?"
(The plagues that Pharaoh and the land of Egypt suffered because they
kept God's people in slavery.)

Turn again to the key question:

What message do you find in this passage for you or for your congregation?

If time permits, consider this additional discussion question:

As you recall the locusts described in Revelation 9:3-10, can you think of some demonic "locusts" that afflict society today?

Close with an appropriate prayer, containing ideas such as the following:

God almighty and all-powerful, throughout your Word and throughout history we see your power overcoming your enemies. They can do great harm, but cannot avoid your verdict and your vengeance. How grateful we are that, though at times we have turned against you and lived in defiance of your will, yet your great mercy invites us back to your forgiveness and your friendship. Forgive now whatever we confess to you in silence, and restore us with your steadfast love to the company of your people.

LESSON SIX

PURPOSE

To see that beyond the symbolism and code language of the Book of Revelation, God's righteousness and love require the possibility of eternal condemnation because God respects our free will and never forces us to repent.

SUGGESTED PROCEDURE

Write on chalkboard or poster board the following questions:

How is the woman described?
What is expected of the son she bears?
Who wants to destroy the child?
Where is the child taken for safety?

Ask half the group to read silently Matthew 2:1-21. Ask the others to read silently Revelation 12:1-9. Ask each group to report how the passage they read answers the above questions. Without implying that the author of Revelation has deliberately used Matthew's account of Jesus' birth as a pattern, compare the answers.

Ask the group to turn to *Breaking the Code*, page 72. Notice what Dr. Metzger has to say about the relationship between these two radically different passages of Scripture.

If you are using the video lessons, at this time allow
17 minutes to watch Video Lesson Six.

Ask members of the class to think about how many numbers that they need for identification in our society. Some will be able to tell their auto license number, Social Security number, phone number, nine-digit zip code, and perhaps others. Offer to give them an additional personal number, a number representing their name.

Use the chalkboard or newsprint to explain that the letters of the Greek alphabet, in sets of ten, also served as numerals. Tell the class that if each letter of the English alphabet had an equivalent number the pattern might be something like this:

A = 1	J = 10	S = 100
B = 2	K = 20	T = 200
C = 3	L = 30	U = 300
D = 4	M = 40	V = 400
E = 5	N = 50	W = 500
F = 6	O = 60	X = 600
G = 7	P = 70	Y = 700
H = 8	Q = 80	Z = 800
I = 9	R = 90	

Make clear to the class that the list is an approximation only; in English there are no equivalents between our alphabet and our numerical system. Spell a few names of class members and add the numbers represented by each letter to illustrate the idea. Use the names William and Marcia for examples:

W =	500		M =	40
I =	9		A =	1
L =	30		R =	90
L =	30		C =	3
I =	9		I =	9
A =	1		A =	1
M =	40			
	619			144

Learners may enjoy and remember the activity if they try to determine a number for their own name or the name of some famous person now living.

Ask class members what they have heard about the number 666. Many persons seem to believe that number to be a mystery central to the Book of Revelation. Ask if anyone can suggest a reason why 666 would be so important. Why hasn't equal importance been given to dozens of other symbols in Revelation? Ask the group to name some of the other symbols used by John, such as the lampstands that are the seven churches or the vision of the New Jerusalem.

To see 666 as a numerical representation of a name (possibly Nero Caesar or "Neron" Caesar) takes away some of the mystery. Remembering how the writer of the Book of Revelation has used numbers elsewhere, consider 144,000. In Revelation 7:5-8 we see that a thousand, a number suggesting completeness, is multiplied by 12, the number of the tribes of Israel, and again by 12. Twelve is also the number of Jesus' apostles. Ask, "Will God's redeemed sons and daughters be counted so that after 143,999 only one more will be accepted, and everyone else excluded?" Remind the group that most often in the Book of Revelation numbers are symbols, not to be taken literally.

Apply the key question to today's lesson.

What message do you find in this part of the Book of Revelation for you or for your congregation?

Close the lesson with a prayer such as:

> **God of grace and God of judgment, we are a part of humankind. Our actions as individuals have too often failed to recognize or stand against corporate and global wrongs. The power of evil has overwhelmed our feeble calls for charity and justice. But you, O God, are greater than the forces that oppose you. Help us know how to trust you, to be faithful to your purposes, and to wait for your time of judgment.**

LESSON SEVEN

PURPOSE

To see in the increasingly intense calamity and terror of the Book of Revelation the need for God's faithful servants to be prepared for long and bitter suffering without allowing discouragement or doubt to destroy their faith.

SUGGESTED PROCEDURE

Write on the chalkboard the five Bible references that follow. Assign to each member of the group one or more of these passages, all of which are songs:

Revelation 5:13-14; 7:11-12; 11:16; 12:10-12; 15:3-4.

Ask group members to read aloud these songs. Point out that the tense dramatic action of John's visions is periodically relieved by these songs of praise. This great poetry has often influenced anthems and musical works such as Handel's *Messiah*.

Write the word *Babylon* on the chalkboard or on a sheet of paper taped where all class members can see it. Ask, "What did this word probably mean to the original readers of Revelation?"

At this point use 16 minutes to show Video Lesson Seven.

When the tape is finished, ask everyone to turn in their Bibles to chapter 18 of Revelation. Suggest that learners look for similar words in verses 10, 16, and 19 ("Alas, alas, the great city"). Call attention to the name of the city, Babylon, found in verses 2, 10, and 21. Babylon, whose military power had conquered Judah six centuries earlier, had long ago passed into history for the original readers of the Book of Revelation. Suggest to your group members that "Babylon" in Revelation is probably a code word (for Rome).

Ask class members to find page 88 in *Breaking the Code*. Ask what Dr. Metzger sees in the term *Babylon* as allegorical for today. (ways that nations create idols: material abundance; military prowess; technological sophistication; imperial grandeur; and racial pride)

In each case national accomplishments are falsely considered greater than the One who created the nations. Ask for examples of each of the five, either from past history or from the present time.

Direct the discussion from forms of national idolatry to another statement near the end of the video lesson: "To the extent that ecclesiastical denominations have also succumbed to the lure of power and prestige, the words of John are applicable also to present-day church structures."

Ask how many agree that religious organizations sometimes elevate their bureaucracies, traditions, and leaders so that creatures come before the Creator. Discuss how the church could avoid receiving the wrath of God. (Possible answers might include giving more importance to the Bible, to repentence, or to reformation.)

POINTERS FOR LEADERS:
REVELATION IN SONG

Some of the best-loved music of the church is based on parts of the Book of Revelation. You may wish to sing, to listen to, and/or to examine the texts of some of these:

"The Battle Hymn of the Republic," by Julia Ward Howe (Revelation 14:17-20)

"Holy, Holy, Holy," by Reginald Heber (Revelation 4)

"The Holy City," by Adolphe Adam (Revelation 21 and 22)

"The Hallelujah Chorus" from *Messiah*, by George Frederick Handel (Revelation 11:15; 19;1,7)

Close the lesson with prayer, perhaps using these words:

O God whom we worship when two or three or thousands gather in the name of Christ, we thank you for the church, which in spite of human pride and selfishness shows us a path to follow. Cleanse all who gather in your name, so that we may ask to be a forgiven and faithful people. Where it must be, make us able to accept your judgment and help us bravely bear suffering through the example of your son Jesus Christ.

LESSON EIGHT

PURPOSE

To review the symbolic content of the Book of Revelation as a message intended to show God's power as permanent, leading toward triumph in a new world where suffering and sorrow are ended and faithful Christians enter an eternal relationship of closeness to God.

SUGGESTED PROCEDURE

Ask group members to find in their Bibles two of the best-known passages in the Book of Revelation, 21:1-7 and 22:1-5. Select a good reader to read each of these passages aloud.

At this point use Video Lesson Eight, allowing 18 minutes.

Today you need to draw to a conclusion the entire eight-part video study. Remind the class members that the key question you have been using has both a personal and a corporate focus. State the question in two forms:

What message do you find in today's passage for you or for your congregation? What is the value of the entire Book of Revelation for your personal faith and for the life of your congregation?

Ask class members to find page 92 in *Breaking the Code* and see how the teaching of the Qumram sect differed from John's account in Revelation. (Victory over evil needed the military help of the faithful according to the teachings of the Qumran sect. In Revelation human help isn't needed; Christ's Word is sufficient.)

If time permits, consider these additional discussion questions:

In Romans 13:4 Paul writes about the state as God's servant. In the Book of Revelation John seems to cast the state in a different light. How would you explain the difference?

Why would John portray the glory of heaven in terms of a city?

Call upon group members each to offer a sentence prayer if that is appropriate. Or, you might offer the following prayer:

We thank you, O God, for the new insights you have given us as we have thought about the Book of Revelation. There is still much that we do not understand. The more we know the more we disagree with some of our fellow Christians. Even so, we pray that our love may increase toward them as we recognize your love reaching out to all of us. Continue to keep us growing, we pray in the name of Christ.

POINTERS FOR LEADERS: SIMULTANEOUS MESSAGES

Leander Keck, in his book *The Church Confident* (Abingdon, 1993; pages 101-103), points out how the way persons communicate bears on the Book of Revelation:

"In reading, as in writing, communication is sequential . . . one follows the text from beginning to end. . . . In viewing a painting or a piece of sculpture, however, the communication is simultaneous as the eye takes in form, line, color, and composition all at once, even if one looks at parts of the work.

"The difference becomes even more obvious when one reads a description of a work of art. Then one discovers that the sequence of words and sentences cannot communicate what strikes the eye simultaneously because one can write and read only one thing at a time. In my work as a teacher of the New Testament, repeatedly this phenomenon has frustrated my efforts to teach the Book of Revelation, where a sequence of words tries to convey what sometimes the seer saw simultaneously. . . .

"Today's technology has made it possible for the combination of sound, image, and words to communicate a quite different power. In music video, powerful rhythms and sounds merge with swiftly moving images accompanied by words in order to offer an experience of participation by resonating with the performance. In terms of communicating, the contrast between silent reading and vibrating with MTV could hardly be greater. If reading appeals to reason and reflection, MTV appeals to emotion and immediacy."

Music videos can be seen on the MTV channel, available through cable telecasting. MTV's popularity with youth and young adults often befuddles the older generation, but might well be useful in understanding Revelation. If you are not familiar with MTV, find an opportunity to watch for awhile. First, turn the sound completely off. Then increase the volume slowly.

Another example of cumulative rather than sequential communication is the three-ring circus. Lions and tigers, musicians, clowns, trapeze artists, and even hucksters selling popcorn play their parts at the same time, giving the audience a total immersion in the experience.

Can we create a similar impact with the Book of Revelation? Try reading aloud. Practice it to add dramatic changes of speed and inflection. Then read it to one or more other persons.

Revelation 1:3 tells us the author expected this Scripture to be read aloud, reaching others through the ears. There are countless paintings based on the words of John of Patmos, usually incorporating much detail. Works of art make their own impact on attempts to understand Revelation, but oral reading works much like old-time radio and allows the hearer to form pictures in the mind.

Expanding This Study
Into A Thirteen-Week Quarter

1. "An Introduction for Today"
Use Video Lesson One and Metzger, chapter 1. Browse through the
entire Book of Revelation. *See pages 4-6, this guide.*

2. "The Original Introduction"
Use Revelation 1:1-20 and Metzger, chapter 2. Do not use the video
this time. *See pages 4-6, this guide.*

3. "Messages to Churches"
Use Revelation 2:1-29, Video Lesson Two, and Metzger, chapter 3.
See pages 7-9, this guide.

4. "More Messages to Churches"
Use Revelation 3:1-22 and Metzger, chapter 4. Do not use the video
this time. *See pages 7-9, this guide.*

5. "God and the Lamb"
Use Revelation 4:1—5:14, Video Lesson Three, and Metzger,
chapter 5. *See pages 10-11, this guide.*

6. "Seven Seals on the Scroll"
Use Revelation 6:1—8:4, Video Lesson Four, and Metzger, chapter
6. *See pages 12-14, this guide.*

7. "Seven Trumpets"
Use Revelation 8:5—11:19, Video Lesson Five, and Metzger,
chapter 7. *See pages 15-16, this guide.*

8. "The Dragon and Two Beasts"
Use Revelation 12:1—13:18, Video Lesson Six, and first part of
Metzger, chapter 8 as far as "Begin with the following chapter."
See pages 17-19, this guide.

9. "The 144,000"
Use Revelation 14:1-20 and last part of Metzger, chapter 8 from
"Begin with the following chapter." Do not use the video this time.
See pages 17-19, this guide.

10. "Armageddon"

Use Revelation 15:1— 16:21, Video Lesson Seven, and first part of Metzger, chapter 9 as far as "Finally the seventh angel." *See pages 20-21, this guide.*

11. "The Mysterious Babylon"

Use Revelation 17:1—18:24 and last part of Metzger, chapter 9 beginning with "Finally the seventh angel." Do not use the video this time. *See pages 20-21, this guide.*

12. "Death and Judgment"

Use Revelation 19:1—20:15 and Metzger, chapter 10. Do not use the video this time. *See pages 22-24, this guide.*

13. "New Heaven and New Earth"

Use Revelation 21:1— 22:21, Video Lesson Eight, and Metzger, chapter 11. *See pages 22-24, this guide.*

Condensing This Study Into Four Lessons

For those classes unable to spend eight hours studying Dr. Metzger's video presentations and his book, *Breaking the Code*, four lessons will provide a brief introduction to these resources. Participants should be urged to keep up with the suggested readings from *Breaking the Code* and from the Bible.

For a four-week series, allow two video lessons each week, with brief discussion time between

LESSON ONE (4-WEEK PLAN)

Materials for Advance Reading: *Breaking the Code*, chapters 1—4
    Revelation 1:1—3:22

Give a brief introduction.
Use Video Lesson One.
Select an activity from pages 4-6 of this guide. Follow the activity with Video Lesson Two.
Discuss a question from page 8 of this guide.
Close with prayer from page 6.

LESSON TWO (4-WEEK PLAN)

Materials for Advance Reading:
    Breaking the Code, chapters 5 and 6
    Revelation 4:1—8:4

Give a brief introduction.
Use Video Lesson Three.
Select an activity from pages 10-11 of this guide.
Use Video Lesson Four.
Discuss pages 12-14 of this guide.
Close with prayer from page 14.

LESSON THREE (4-WEEK PLAN)

Materials for Advance Reading:
    Breaking the Code, chapters 7 and 8
    Revelation 8:5—14:20

Give a brief introduction.
Use Video Lesson Five.
Select an activity from pages 15-16 of this guide.
Use Video Lesson Six.
Discuss pages 18-19 of this guide.
Close with prayer from page 19.

LESSON FOUR (4-WEEK PLAN)
Materials for Advance Reading:
Breaking the Code, chapters 9—11
Revelation 15:1—22:21

Give a brief introduction.
Use Video Lesson Seven.
Select an activity from pages 20-21 of this guide.
Use Video Lesson Eight.
Discuss a question from pages 22-23 of this guide.
Close with a prayer from page 23.

FEWER THAN FOUR LESSONS
Do not attempt to show more than two video lessons at one time. (Even when two are shown, a different activity inserted between the two is recommended.)

Use Video Lesson One with a group that wants a one-time presentation.

Bibliography—
If You Want To Learn More

Various points of view are found in the books listed below. Some additional volumes are included in a list on pages 107 and 108 of *Breaking the Code*.

Barclay, William. *The Revelation of John*, 2 volumes. Philadelphia: Westminster Press, 1976. A useful commentary, primarily for lay people.

Boring, M. Eugene. *Revelation*. Louisville: Westminster John Knox Press, 1989. A volume in the series, *Interpretation, A Bible Commentary for Teaching and Preaching*.

Caird, George B. *The Revelation of St. John the Divine*. New York: Harper & Row, 1966. A standard, verse-by-verse commentary.

Clouse, Robert G., ed. *The Meaning of the Millennium*. Downers Grove, Illinois: InterVarsity Press, 1977. Four authors discuss the main views of the millennium (Revelation 20).

Ewert, David. *The Church Under Fire*. Hillsboro, Kansas: Kindred Press, 1988. A helpful and balanced exposition, with present-day applications.

Grenz, Stanley J. *The Millenial Maze: Sorting Out Evangelical Options*. Downers Grove, Illinois: InterVarsity, 1992.

Jeffrey, D.L., ed. *A Dictionary of Biblical Tradition in English Literature*. Grand Rapids, Michigan: Wm. B. Eerdmans Publishing Co., 1992. Draws connections between scenes described in Revelation and contemporary literature.

Jewett, Robert. *Jesus Against the Rapture: Seven Unexpected Prophecies*. Philadelphia: Westminster Press, 1979. A response to the perspective found in various popular books by Hal Lindsey.

Stott, John R. W. *What Christ Thinks of the Church*. Wheaton, Illinois: Shaw Publishers, 1990. Deals with Revelation 1—3.

Wainwright, Arthur. *Mysterious Apocalypse: Interpreting the Book of Revelation*. Atlanta: Abingdon Press, 1993. Contains different representations of art based on the Apocalypse.

Revelation's Seven Beatitudes

Blessed is the one who reads aloud the words of the prophecy, and blessed are those who hear and who keep what is written in it; for the time is near. (1:3)

Blessed are the dead who from now on die in the Lord. "Yes," says the Spirit, "they will rest from their labors, for their deeds from their labors, for their deeds follow them." (14:13)

Blessed is the one who stays awake and is clothed, not going about naked and exposed to shame. (16:15)

Blessed are those who are invited to the marriage supper of the lamb. (19:9)

Blessed and holy are those who share in the first resurrection. Over these the second death has no power, but they will be priests of God and of Christ, and they will reign with him a thousand years. (20:6)

Blessed is the one who keeps the words of the prophecy of this book. (22:7)

Blessed are those who wash their robes, so that they will have the right to the tree of life and may enter the city by the gates. (22:14)

Art and Photographs
Used in *Breaking the Code* Video

John on Patmos—Burgkmair, Hans the Elder (Scala/Art Resource)
Gladiators and Lion—Henri Rousseau—The Detroit Institute of Arts
Emperor Domitian—Art Resource
American Eagle—Copyright © Byron Jorjorian
Soldier/British Lion/Donkey & Elephant—Copyright © 1993
    Abingdon Press
Jim Jones/David Koresh—Religious News Service
The Adoration of the Holy Lamb—(Van Eyck) Art Resource
Sun in Red Sky—Copyright © Jim Whitmer
Rainbow—Copyright © 1992 Cokesbury
Vision of Eziekel—(Raphael) Art Resource
Jesus' Entry to Jerusalem—Art Resource
The Vision of St. John—(Memling) Art Resource
Child in Somalia—Copyright © Jim Whitmer
Opening the 6th Seal—(Danby) Copyright The National Gallery of
    Ireland
Red Sky and Ocean—Copyright © Jim Whitmer
Julius Ceasar—Art Resource
John on Patmos—(Bosch) State Museums, Berlin
Nazi Propaganda Poster— Art Resource
Shots of Jewish Prisoners—The National Archives and Records
    Administration
The Last Judgement—(Michelangelo) Art Resource
Plains of Heaven—(John Martin) Tate Gallery, London

CPSIA information can be obtained
at www.ICGtesting.com
Printed in the USA
LVOW07s0145031117
554811LV00008B/38/P